AF207198

CAMPING

By Donna B. McKinney

SportsZone

An Imprint of Abdo Publishing
abdobooks.com

abdobooks.com

Published by Abdo Publishing, a division of ABDO, PO Box 398166, Minneapolis, Minnesota 55439. Copyright © 2020 by Abdo Consulting Group, Inc. International copyrights reserved in all countries. No part of this book may be reproduced in any form without written permission from the publisher. SportsZone™ is a trademark and logo of Abdo Publishing.

Printed in the United States of America, North Mankato, Minnesota
092019
012020

Cover Photo: Shutterstock images
Interior Photos: Feel Good Studio/Shutterstock Images, 5; Corbis Historical/Getty Images, 7; Iryna Inshyna/Shutterstock Images, 8; Shutterstock Images, 10–11, 18, 21, 30, 37, 38, 45; iStockphoto, 13; Light Field Studios/Shutterstock Images, 14; Svitlana Pimenov/Shutterstock Images, 17; Florida Stock/Shutterstock Images, 22; Red Line Editorial, 25; Ken Wolter/Shutterstock Images, 26–27; Jens Ottoson/Shutterstock Images, 29; Iakov Filimonov/Shutterstock Images, 33; Press Lab/Shutterstock Images, 34; Kimberly Boyles/Shutterstock Images, 41; Anusorn Thongpasan/Shutterstock Images, 42

Editor: Patrick Donnelly
Series Designer: Colleen McLaren

Library of Congress Control Number: 2019941981

Publisher's Cataloging-in-Publication Data

Names: McKinney, Donna B., author
Title: Camping / by Donna B. McKinney
Description: Minneapolis, Minnesota : Abdo Publishing, 2020 | Series: Outdoor adventures | Includes online resources and index
Identifiers: ISBN 9781532190476 (lib. bdg.) | ISBN 9781532176326 (ebook)
Subjects: LCSH: Camping--Juvenile literature. | Outdoor recreation--Juvenile literature. | Wilderness areas--Visitors--Juvenile literature. | Camping areas--Juvenile literature.
Classification: DDC 796.54--dc23

TABLE OF
CONTENTS

CHAPTER 1

LET'S GO CAMPING

The two sisters carefully stack the firewood. Crisscross, crisscross, they lay the wood until it looks like a tiny log cabin. Their younger brother drops tiny twigs and dry, crunchy leaves on top of the logs they stacked. "It's ready!" he cries. Their mother lights the campfire while their father prepares the hot dogs and vegetables for cooking.

Soon everyone is eating, surrounded by the sounds of the woods. The stream just beyond their tent gurgles. The endless chirps of crickets rise out of the woods. And their campfire hisses and pops as the logs burn down to just a glow. The stresses of city life are the furthest thing from their minds at the moment. Camping is their favorite kind of vacation.

A good campfire is an important part of camping.

THE FATHER OF CAMPING

In 1869 William H. H. Murray, a young minister, wrote a how-to book about camping called *Adventures in the Wilderness; or, Camp-Life in the Adirondacks*. Today *Smithsonian Magazine* calls Murray the "minister who invented camping in America."

In his book, Murray suggested that camping is good for people both physically and spiritually. People read the book, and they soon headed into the woods to camp. Americans embraced this new outdoor activity.

Before Murray wrote his camping book, a few hundred people visited New York's Adirondack Mountains each summer. Soon after people started reading his book, those numbers rose to 2,000 to 3,000 camping in the Adirondacks. Many of them were carrying copies of Murray's book.

At the time, women were not often included in outdoor activities. But Murray proposed that women would enjoy camping too. He wrote that camping

Americans have been camping for recreation since the late 1800s.

was "delightful to ladies. There is nothing in the trip which the most delicate and fragile need fear."

Murray's book was similar to many camping guides today. It told people how to get to the Adirondack Mountains, how to set up camp, and what gear to pack.

But his book was unique because it also described camping as a pilgrimage. Murray said living in busy, crowded cities caused people to become confused

Relaxing in the outdoors provides many health benefits.

and anxious. Going away to spend time in nature was healing for a person's soul, he wrote. Americans' interest in camping was forever changed by Murray's book. Because of it, generations of people left the city and headed out into the woods.

CAMPING'S MANY BENEFITS

Campers today enjoy these same kinds of benefits that those early campers in the late 1800s discovered. Researchers have found that spending time in the forest lowers the stress hormone cortisol that is found in the human body. It also lowers a person's heart rate and blood pressure. Camping can calm a person and help ease feelings of stress.

Camping helps reset the body clock. Spending most of the time indoors confuses the body's internal clock and can affect how well a person sleeps. Being out in the bright sunlight, with less light at night, helps campers sleep well and wake up less groggy. Camping also helps boost the immune system. This means the body is better able to fight off sickness and disease.

HAMMOCK CAMPING

Some campers swap their tents for hammocks. Instead of a sleeping bag and tent, they choose to sleep in a hammock strung between two trees. Lightweight and sturdy hammocks are made specifically for camping. They feature tarps to guard against rain and bug nets to ward off insects.

Hammock camping has become a popular activity.

"Camping is like a mental massage," says Hope Oldham, a senior REI Outdoor School instructor. "Even on the trips where everything goes wrong, you come home feeling refreshed and reinvigorated."

Camping is a great all-around workout. And it is fun for people of all ages. So gather the gear, load up the backpack, and head into the great outdoors.

CHAPTER 2

BEFORE YOU GO

Before heading out into the woods, it's important to do some research and make sound plans for the trip. Campers have many decisions to make before they go.

For example, they need to decide whether to rent or purchase their gear. Camping equipment can be expensive, especially the big items such as tents and sleeping bags. Some campers rent this gear instead of buying it. Businesses that sell outdoor gear can be good places to rent camping gear. Renting can be smart for beginning campers. It lets them try out different kinds of gear before committing the money to buy it.

It's important to know what gear to pack before you go camping.

WHAT TO WEAR

The best clothes for camping help people stay
dry. This means campers should leave cotton
clothes, such as jeans and T-shirts, at home.
Cotton holds moisture—sweat or rain—close to
the body. This is uncomfortable and even chilly in

cooler temperatures. The best camping clothes are polyester, nylon, or wool fabrics. Activewear or sportswear clothes are usually made of these materials because they allow for quick drying.

Campers also like to dress in layers. That allows them to take off a shirt as it gets warmer or add a sweater if the temperature drops. Even during warm summer months, nighttime temperatures can be chilly. So it is smart to bring plenty of warm clothes for the cool nights.

A rain jacket is an important piece to pack. It can protect the camper against wind and rain. In cooler weather, campers should bring a warm jacket and gloves along with the rain jacket.

To protect their feet, campers can wear hiking boots or trail shoes. The key is to choose shoes that support the feet and grip the trail well in wet or dry weather. Extra socks are important to prevent blisters.

In all kinds of weather, a wide-brimmed hat and sunglasses help protect a camper from the sun. It is smart to remember that the clothes they bring will probably end up smoky, wet, and dirty. So campers should avoid packing anything too delicate for the outdoors.

WHAT TO EAT

Depending on a camper's cooking skills, camp meals can range from simple to fancy. The food choices should be easy to prepare using a campfire or camp stove. Sausages, hotdogs, and burgers are easy to prepare over a fire. A camp breakfast of bacon and eggs is a great way to start the day. But instant oatmeal or dried cereal also work for campers looking for simple food choices.

Campers like to carry plenty of snacks because being in the outdoors hiking and playing makes everyone hungry. Trail mix, nuts, granola bars, dried fruits, and vegetables all make good snacks for camping.

Some people like to prepare elaborate meals while camping.

Campers often enjoy meals that can be prepared in one pot, such as chilis, stews, or pasta dishes. With just one pot, the preparation, cooking, and cleanup can be simpler. Carrying foods in jars or cans creates a heavy load in a camper's backpack. Packing foods in sealed plastic bags can help lighten the weight load.

WATCH THE WEATHER

Going camping often means getting wet and muddy. Campers can wear rain gear or stay inside their tent when it is raining. But thunderstorms can be dangerous. It is wise for campers to follow the weather forecast and try to avoid being outdoors during thunderstorms. There is no safe place outdoors during a thunderstorm.

PRACTICE AT HOME

Some campers are able to practice setting up the tent the first time in their own backyard. A practice run at home lets campers be sure they have the necessary tools for a successful setup while they are close to their house and not in the woods.

When campers arrive at an actual campsite, they look for dry, level ground to pitch the tent. As much as possible, the ground should be clear of sticks and other debris that might punch a hole in the tent. Setting up the tent so that its back is to the wind helps make it stable.

WHERE TO CAMP

People have a wide variety of places to choose from when deciding where to go camping. Some campers prefer to be completely cut off from the rest of the world—no electricity, no running water, no sign of human life within miles. Others might prefer a less rustic environment where they can enjoy the peace and tranquility of nature without sacrificing too many of the comforts and conveniences of home.

Site selection also depends on the activities campers are hoping to take part in. Boating enthusiasts will look for destinations with access to lakes or rivers. People who like to hike might check out maps of local trails before choosing a site.

There are many ways to go camping, from very rustic to comfortable and modern.

Campers in parks can visit the ranger's station if they need assistance.

Regardless of campers' preferences, there are great places to camp all across the country.

CLOSE TO HOME

Most campers suggest that beginning campers plan their first trip at a location near their home. If a camper forgets something or has some unexpected problems while camping, being closer to home means the solutions can be close at hand. With a little camping experience near home, campers can then venture out to camp in more remote places.

PUBLIC LANDS

The US government has set aside land throughout the country for public use. The Recreation.gov website is a great resource for campers who might want to visit these federal lands, which are located throughout the country in all types of terrain. This website helps campers plan their trips and make reservations, if they are needed. It also features information about fishing, hunting, horseback riding, and boating.

NATIONAL AND STATE PARKS

With more than 60 locations to choose from in the United States, national parks can be a great choice for campers. At national parks, campsites can be found in forests, in deserts, or on beaches. Some sites are near rivers and oceans. From Alaska to Hawaii or from Maine to the Virgin Islands, parklands provide great places to camp. Campers can explore the National Park Service website to learn about the various parks and what they have to offer.

Like national parks, state parks can be a great choice for campers too. No matter which of the 50 states a camper lives in, there will be campgrounds close to home. More than 8,000 state park areas and 200,000 campsites provide plenty of options for camping in a state park. The campgrounds range from primitive sites far from civilization to cozy cabins and cottages available to rent.

WILDERNESS AREAS

Wilderness areas that are protected by the federal government can be great places to camp. The Bureau of Land Management, Fish and Wildlife Service, Forest Service, and National Park Service all work together to manage wilderness areas. Besides camping, people enjoy hiking, canoeing, rafting, swimming, fishing, hunting, and climbing in wilderness areas. There are 803 wilderness areas across the United States. California, Arizona, Nevada, Alaska, and Oregon have the most sites.

—US NATIONAL PARKS—

The United States has designated more than 60 recreational areas as national parks. They stretch from coast to coast and even beyond—there's a national park in the US Virgin Islands and another one in American Samoa (not shown on map).

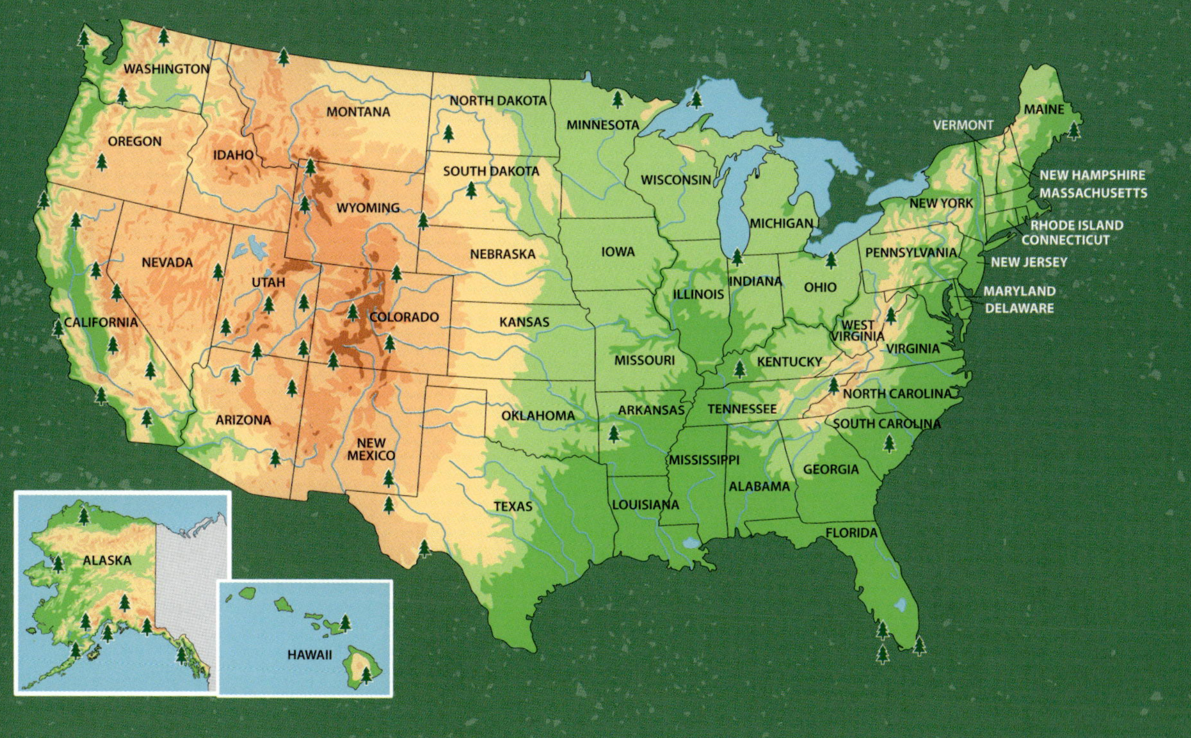

CAMPGROUNDS

Public and private campgrounds across the country give campers a range of options. For example, Kampgrounds of America (KOA) is a large system

KOA campgrounds are found all over North America.

of private campgrounds with almost 500 locations across the United States and Canada.

The experience at this type of campground can vary depending on how rustic the campers want to make it. Some offer just the basics of a simple campsite. Other campgrounds might offer showers and toilets or even a place to do laundry. Some campgrounds offer activities for campers. And some

offer wireless internet service so campers can stay connected while they camp. Campers should decide what kind of camping trip they want and then do their research before they head off to the woods.

PRIMITIVE CAMPING

In primitive camping, campers carry backpacks containing everything they need to survive in the woods. They camp far from facilities, with no electricity, running water, or bathrooms. Primitive camping is sometimes called backcountry camping.

CHAPTER 4

ALL THE GEAR

Camping does require a fair amount of gear. Campers have to eat, sleep, and live in the woods. That can mean carrying a lot of supplies in a backpack. The supply list can vary depending on the length and location of the trip. But one of the most important considerations is their home away from home.

TENTS

Choosing the size of tent that fits a camper's needs is important. "Bigger is better" is not always true. The size and weight of the tent really matter to backpackers, who must carry the tent from site to site. Even campers traveling in cars want to choose the right tent for their camping needs.

Campers should find the type of tent that suits their needs.

The size and weight of your tent will depend on where and when you are camping.

Tents come in a wide range of sizes and styles. Heavier tents are made for colder temperatures. Other tents are lighter in weight, but they're not meant for extreme temperatures. Pop-up tents, dome tents, and tunnel tents are just a few of the popular tents campers enjoy using.

A tent is usually rated for its capacity—how many campers it will hold. Before campers head to the woods, it is smart to check and be sure the tallest person in the group can sit up and stretch out inside the tent.

Some tents can be divided into two rooms. This style of tent can be a nice option when several people are sharing the same space.

Back home after the camping trip, campers often set up the tent outside on a breezy, sunny day. Any dampness from rain or just being in the woods can dry before the tent is packed up for storage.

SLEEPING BAGS

Just like tents, campers can choose from many types of sleeping bags. Those sleeping in colder temperatures at night will want a heavier bag. A sleeping bag is rated by the temperatures in which it can keep the camper warm. This might be listed as a "comfort rating"—the temperature at which a camper might be comfortable. It could also be listed as a "lower-limit rating"—the lowest temperature at which a camper might feel warm.

Campers who have had a hard day hiking or doing other outdoor activities might not notice the hard ground beneath their sleeping bag. But most campers like to use a sleeping pad underneath their sleeping bag. Sleeping pads are made of foam or filled with air and placed between the sleeping bag and the ground. They give an extra boost of comfort.

CAMPSITE COOKING

Campers can work up big appetites, so it's important to carry the right gear for cooking. Some campers prefer to cook over an open fire. But many campers bring a small stove for preparing their food.

Campers like to plan their meals carefully and carry

A good sleeping bag can keep a camper warm even on the coldest nights.

just enough pots, pans, and dishes to get the job done. Extra pots and pans can be a burden to carry. Pots and pans from the kitchen at home can work for camping meals. Camping stores and outdoor sports stores also sell cookware made for camping. Camping cookware is lightweight and made for easy packing.

A GPS device works well if there's a strong signal in the wilderness.

Access to safe drinking water is another necessity, especially in hot weather. Too much heat and not enough water can be a recipe for heat-related illnesses. Some campgrounds have fresh water available for campers. But that is not always an option. Campers can carry a water filtration system or iodine tablets to treat the water they find. Water that looks clear still might not be safe to drink.

TOOLS FOR CAMPING

Campers usually bring basic tools for the chores around the campsite, such as setting up the tent or building the campfire. These tools might include matches, a simple pocketknife, an ax, a hammer, or a knife with extra tools attached.

Some campers use a Global Positioning System (GPS) device to help them find their way in the woods. But cellular service out in the wild can be inconsistent, so it's wise for campers to also know the basics of reading a paper map and a compass. The ranger station can usually provide paper maps of the area. And it gets dark out in the woods. Headlamps, flashlights, and lanterns help light the way after the sun goes down.

SAFETY FIRST

Experienced campers know and follow safety rules. These rules help to keep them safe in the woods. Some of these rules are common sense, but being aware of them can help beginning campers have the best camping trip possible.

THE FIRST AID KIT

Campers need to be prepared for anything that can go wrong. To care for the cuts, bug bites, headaches, and blisters that might happen while camping, a first aid kit is a must-have item in the backpack. A basic kit might include aspirin or ibuprofen, bandages, gauze, tape, antibiotic ointment, tweezers, scissors, cotton-tipped swabs, and moleskin (for blisters).

A first aid kit should be part of every camper's gear.

Campers can build their own kit or buy a premade kit from a camping store or outdoor sports store.

Along with the first aid kit, campers should carry bug spray and sunscreen. It can be a pretty uncomfortable camping trip if those items are left at home. Campers sometimes wear light-colored long-sleeve shirts and long pants to help them see any ticks crawling on them. All campers should check for ticks every day. Also, the Centers for Disease Control recommends that campers check with their doctors to be sure that they are up to date on vaccinations before they go camping.

BE A GOOD NEIGHBOR

Just like when living at home, it's important to be a good neighbor while camping. This means following the park or campground rules. For example, campers are expected to keep the noise down during quiet hours when others are sleeping.

Sunscreen is as important on a camping trip as it is on a trip to the beach.

A clean campsite is another must. At campgrounds, this means making sure all the trash goes to the dumpster each day. In more remote areas, campers pack up their trash and carry it until they reach a place to dispose of it. Campers should abide by the motto "leave no trace." This means they clean up all their trash. They do not disturb the wildlife in any way. They are careful with campfires.

It is especially important for campers to follow campfire rules. If there is a ban against any burning, campers must obey and not build a fire. Some deadly, destructive forest fires have started with a small campfire that simply got out of control.

Campers who bring pets should follow the rules for keeping the animal on a leash and cleaning up after it. Leash rules help both the pet and the wildlife stay safe.

CHECK IN WITH THE RANGER

Campers need to be aware of any severe weather that is headed their way. Park rangers or the people

Campers follow the rules to be respectful to nature and their fellow campers.

in charge at the campground usually have current weather forecasts available. They should be following any weather alerts and know about any warnings for potentially dangerous weather such as lightning or flash floods. They also can alert campers to problems such as rockslides or dangerous wildlife in the area.

Any device used for heating must be kept outside the tent.

TAKE IT OUTSIDE

Campers must never use stoves, heaters, lanterns, or grills—any gear that burns fuel—inside a closed space such as a tent. Carbon monoxide, a gas that has no smell or color, can build up, and it is deadly. For campers trying to stay warm in very cold weather, the solution is to wear extra clothes or grab an extra sleeping bag, not to place a heater or stove inside the tent.

HANDLE FOOD WITH CARE

Campers usually carry their food in waterproof containers. Any food that needs to be kept cold is stored in an insulated cooler to prevent food poisoning. A cooler that works for a picnic might not be the best cooler for camping. While camping, a cooler needs to keep the contents cold for several days, depending on how long the camping trip lasts. Some coolers are even advertised as being bear-proof.

Around the campsite, it is important to keep raw foods stored away from cooked foods. Even though campers are "roughing it" in the wild, they should stay clean by washing their hands and any plates, utensils, or pots used in their cooking. Where there is no water available for washing hands, campers use hand sanitizer.

DON'T FEED THE ANIMALS

Campers should never try to feed or get near wild animals. Wild animals can be dangerous, and some carry diseases that are harmful to campers. The safest bet is for campers to keep their distance.

Campers who leave their food out might attract animals. Food should be packed away in a waterproof container with a tight lid. The food container is then usually stored inside a cooler. Once a meal is over, campers can safely discard all trash in a bag they can carry out of the woods.

Nature can be exciting and beautiful. Camping is an adventurous way to experience the outdoors.

BEAR CANISTERS

Campers need to keep their food (and themselves) safe from hungry animals. A bear canister is a smart way to protect food. These are hard-sided containers used for storing food at campsites. Many national parks require campers to protect their food in bear-resistant containers, also called food lockers or bear boxes.

A bear canister can help protect food from wild animals.

GLOSSARY

carbon monoxide
An odorless, colorless gas that is poisonous to humans.

compass
A tool used for determining true north that is helpful for finding directions in the wilderness.

GPS
Short for Global Positioning System, it uses satellite signals to allow people to determine locations.

hammock
A bed made of fabric or rope suspended between two trees.

iodine tablets
A product used to purify water for drinking.

national parks
Areas across the United States protected by the federal government, allowing people to enjoy the lands and the wildlife within them.

recreational vehicle
A vehicle such as a motor home, pop-up camper, or truck camper that people can use for camping. Also called an RV.

rustic
Plain or simple.

state parks
Recreation areas located in every state in the United States.

wilderness areas
Natural, unsettled lands that are protected by the federal government.

MORE INFORMATION

BOOKS

Colson, Rob. *Ultimate Survival Guide for Kids*. Buffalo, NY: Firefly Books, 2015.

Kuskowski, Alex. *Cool Backyard Camping: Great Things to Do in the Great Outdoors*. Minneapolis, MN: Abdo, 2016.

Winner, Cherie. *Ranger Rick Kids' Guide to Camping: All You Need to Know about Having Fun Outdoors*. Mission Viejo, CA: Walter Foster Jr., 2018.

ONLINE RESOURCES

To learn more about camping, please visit **abdobooklinks.com** or scan this QR code. These links are routinely monitored and updated to provide the most current information available.

INDEX

ABOUT THE AUTHOR

Donna B. McKinney is a writer who lives in North Carolina. She spent many years writing about science and technology topics at the US Naval Research Laboratory in Washington, DC. Now she enjoys writing about topics ranging from science to history to sports for children and young adults. She loves hiking the North Carolina State Parks.